# Treasures

## A Reading/Language Arts Program

Mc Graw Hill **Macmillan McGraw-Hill**

**Contributors**

Time Magazine, Accelerated Reader

learning through listening

Students with print disabilities may be eligible to obtain an accessible, audio version of the pupil edition of this textbook. Please call Recording for the Blind & Dyslexic at I-800-221-4792 for complete information.

A

*The McGraw·Hill Companies*

**Macmillan McGraw-Hill**

Published by Macmillan/McGraw-Hill, of McGraw-Hill Education, a division of The McGraw-Hill Companies, Inc., Two Penn Plaza, New York, New York I0I2I.

Printed in the United States of America

ISBN 0-02-I94634-5/I, Bk. 3

2 3 4 5 6 7 8 9 (07I/043) 09 08 07

# Treasures

## A Reading/Language Arts Program

### Program Authors

Donald R. Bear
Janice A. Dole
Jana Echevarria
Jan E. Hasbrouck
Scott G. Paris
Timothy Shanahan
Josefina V. Tinajero

Mc Graw Hill **Macmillan McGraw-Hill**

## THEME: Being Friends

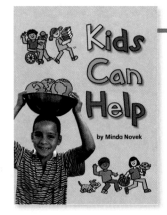

## THEME: Kids Around the World

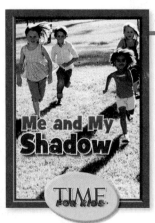

## THEME: Me and My Shadow

# Being Friends

## Talk About It

What do friends do together? How can you be a good friend?

**LOG ON** Find out more about being friends at **www.macmillanmh.com**

## Words to Know

walk

could

all

oh

hello

pull

_____

g<u>a</u>m<u>e</u>

g<u>a</u><u>v</u>e

## Read to Find Out

Will Cat's game be good for all the pals?

# A Good Game for All

by Raymond Storey

illustrated by Daniel Moreton

"Let's **walk** over to see Cat," said Pig
to Frog. "We **could all** play."

"**Oh**, yes," said Frog. "Let's go."

"**Hello**, Pig and Frog," said Cat. "I have a game for us. Let's **pull** on this and see who wins. Frog can pull with me."

Cat and Frog pulled and pulled.
But then Pig gave a big pull, and
down they went!

"This is not a good game for us," said Pig. "Let's play tag."

And that is what they did.

# Comprehension

**Genre**

A fantasy is a made-up story that could not really happen.

**Story Structure**

Make Predictions

As you read, use your **Predictions Chart**.

| What I Predict | What Happens |
|---|---|
|  |  |
|  |  |
|  |  |

**Read to Find Out**

What game will Kate play?

# Kate's Game

by Janie Bynum

Award Winning
**Author**
and
**Illustrator**

Kate liked to make up games. Today, she had her red ball. She tossed it up. It landed on the tip of her trunk.

Tom came to see Kate.

"**Hello**, Kate," he said. "You make up the best games. Can I play, too?"

Kate tossed the ball to Tom.
**PLOP!**
"**Oh**, no!" said Kate. "The ball is in the mud!"

"I **could** get it," said Tom. "Cats are little and fast. We can run on top of mud."

"You are brave," said Kate.

Tom ran to get the ball.

"Oh, no!" said Tom. "The ball is stuck and I am, too."

Jake came to see Kate.

"Hello, Kate," he said. "You make up the best games. Can I play, too?"

"It is not a game," said Kate. "Tom is stuck in the mud."

"I could help," said Jake. "Look at my feet. Ducks can **walk** on mud."

"You are brave," said Kate.

Jake went to help Tom.

"Oh, no!" said Jake. "Tom is stuck and I am, too."

Jane came to see Kate.

"Hello, Kate," she said. "You make up the best games. Can I play, too?"

"It is not a game," said Kate. "Tom and Jake are stuck in the mud."

"I could help," said Jane. "Pigs like mud. I can wade in it."

"You are brave," said Kate.

Jane went to help Jake and Tom.

"Oh, no!" said Jane. "Jake and Tom are stuck and I am, too!"

"I can help," said Kate. "Jane can grab my trunk. Jake can get Jane's tail. Tom can take Jake's wing. Now let's **all pull**."

They all came out of the mud.

"That was not a very good game, Kate," said Tom and Jake and Jane.

"No," said Kate. "But I have a much better one."

"Oh, Kate!" said her friends. "You make up the best games!"

# Janie Bynum's Game

**Janie Bynum** says, "As a child, I was always playing in the mud and making messes. While making messes, I was usually making friends. At the end of the day, we'd spray ourselves with the water hose to get clean."

Other books
by Janie Bynum

Find out more about Janie Bynum at
**www.macmillanmh.com**

## Write About It

Janie Bynum played in the mud. Write about an animal in the story that gets stuck in the mud.

# Comprehension Check

## Retell the Story

Use the Retelling Cards to retell the story.

**Retelling Cards**

## Think and Compare

| What I Predict | What Happens |
|---|---|
|  |  |
|  |  |
|  |  |

1. What did you think Kate's game would be? What really happened?

2. What games do you like to play with friends?

3. How do you know Kate cares about her friends?

4. How are the friends in *Kate's Game* like the friends in "A Good Game For All"?

# When You Mail a Letter

Liz wants to send a letter to her friend Meg.
In the letter, Liz tells Meg about her school.

Liz writes Meg's name and **address**. She adds the **city** and the state. She puts a stamp on it. Then she mails her letter.

A truck will pick it up and take it to a **post office**. At the post office, letters are put into bunches.

Letters going to the same city
go into one bunch. Then a plane
takes Liz's letter away.

Now the letter goes to a post office in Meg's city. A mail carrier gets the letter. She looks at Meg's address.

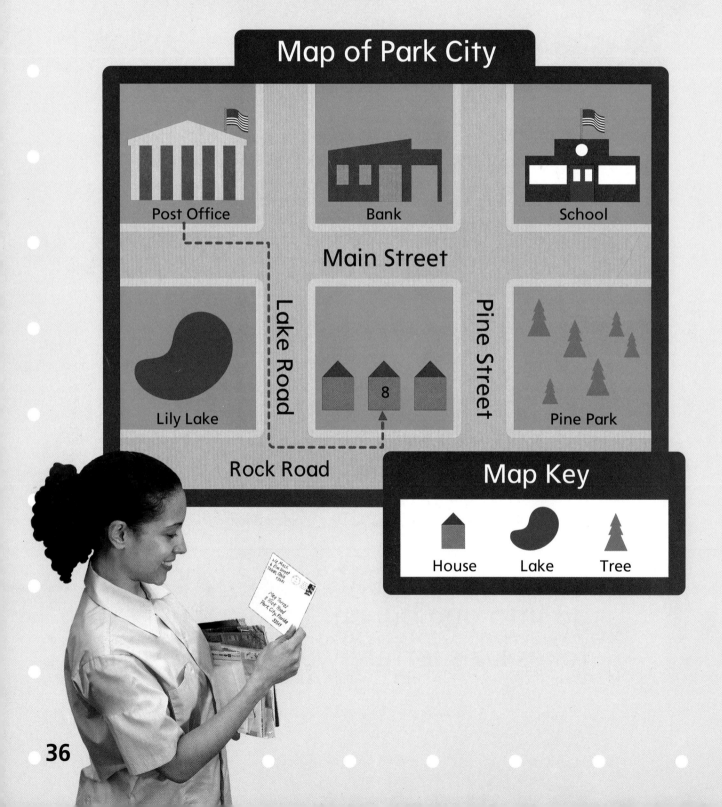

Map of Park City

Post Office

Bank

School

Main Street

Lake Road

Lily Lake

8

Pine Street

Pine Park

Rock Road

Map Key

House    Lake    Tree

Then she brings Meg the letter from her friend!

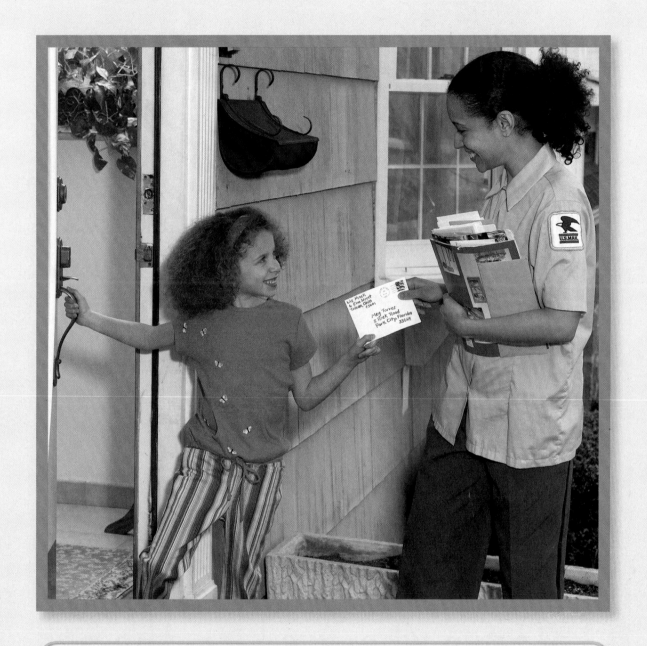

**Connect and Compare**

What might Kate from *Kate's Game* say in a letter to one of her friends?

# Write a Letter

Ramon wrote a letter to a friend about a game.

Dear Greg,

I like playing with you!

It is fun when we kick the ball.

Your friend,
Ramon

38

**ISTEP+** **Writing Activity**

What do you like to do with your friend?

Write a letter to your friend telling about it.

## Writer's Checklist

☑ Did I use different kinds of sentences?

☑ Does each sentence have a verb?

☑ Did I use a comma after the greeting and the closing?

LOG ON

## Talk About It

How are children from other places like you? How are they different?

Find out more about kids around the world at
**www.macmillanmh.com**

# Kids Around the World

## Words to Know

girl
boy
together
when
people
care
water

---

**s**led

**s**wim

 **Read to Find Out**

How do kids around the world play?

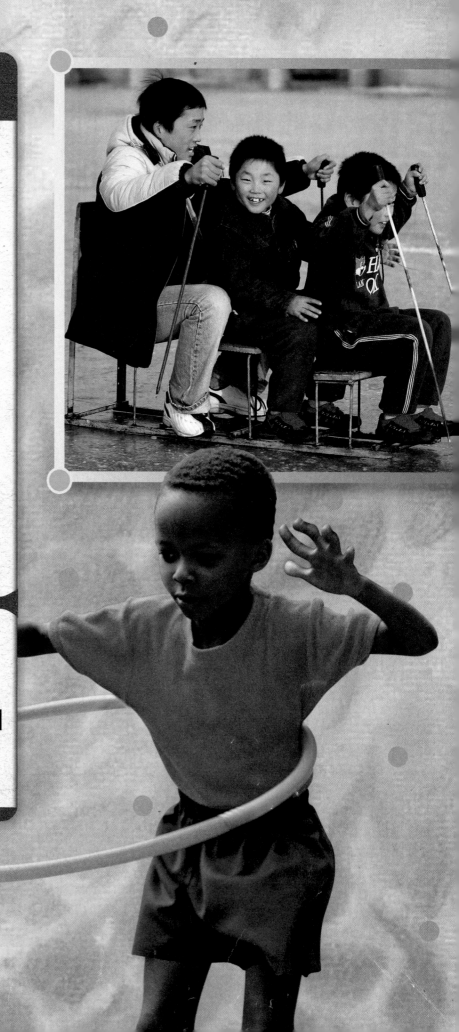

# When Kids Play

## by Linda Ortiz

Kids all over like to play! Look at this **girl** hop. Do you play this game, too?

Kids who live here sled a lot.
This **boy** and girl go down
the hill **together**.

**When** it's hot out, **people** here do not **care**. They can go for a swim. Kids can play in the **water**.

# Kids all over like to play! Do you?

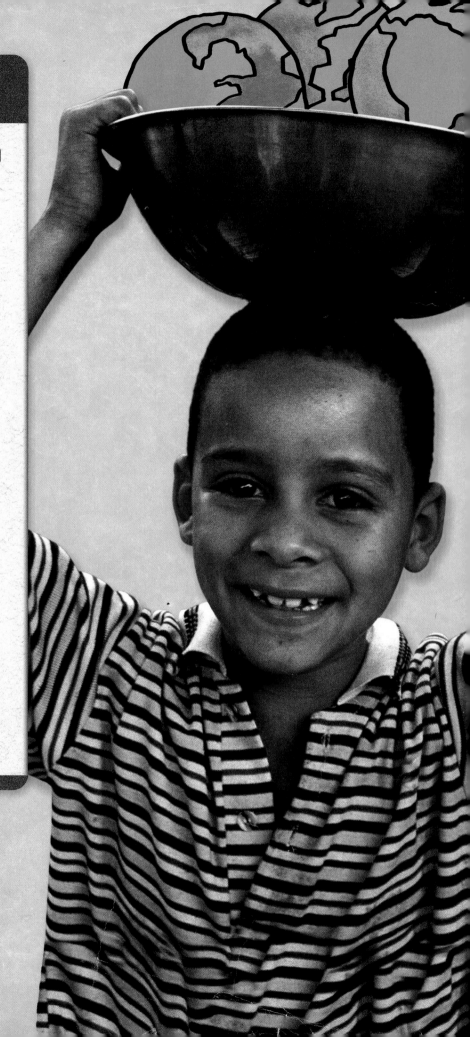

# Comprehension

### Genre
Nonfiction tells about real people and things.

### Text Structure
Compare and Contrast
As you read, use your **Compare and Contrast Chart**.

| Activity | Kids in One Place | Kids in Another Place |
|----------|-------------------|-----------------------|
|          |                   |                       |

### Read to Find Out
How do different kids help their families?

48

# Kids Can Help

by Minda Novek

Kids all over like to help. This **boy** helps his dad cook. **Together** they will make something good to eat.

United States

This **girl** helps her mom bake bread. It smells good. It will taste good, too.

United States

Philippines

Kids can help wash. Where this girl lives, **people** go to the river to wash things. She takes a tub with her.

England

This boy is standing at his sink. He helps wash pots, plates, and cups. He uses **water** and lots of suds.

Where this girl lives, people get water at a well. She will help her mom bring it back home.

Burkina Faso

This boy helps his dad fish. They pick the big ones. Then they take them back home to eat.

Malaysia

United States

This boy takes **care** of his little brother. He helps him to get dressed.

Laos

**When** this girl helps take care of her brother, she puts him on her back.

Here, animals pull big sleds. When they get back home, this girl helps. She takes them to be fed.

Norway

This boy helps take care of animals, too. He takes his llama for a walk.

Peru

Japan

This boy digs and digs. He makes a
safe path. Now his mom and dad
will not slip.

United States

This girl helps take care of the grass. She likes to rake the leaves. Swish, swish, swish!

Kids can help in the neighborhood, too. This boy and girl stack used cans and glass. They will take them to be recycled.

United States

This boy helps take care of plants.
He brings them water to drink.

Kids all over like to help! Do you?

United States

# Minda Novek's World

**Minda Novek** says, "In my books, I like to write about how people live all over the world. I use pictures of real people. I try to show how their lives are like yours and how they are different, too."

**LOG ON** Find out more about Minda Novek at **www.macmillanmh.com**

## Write About It

Minda Novek wrote about how kids help. Show how you help. Write about your picture.

64

## Comprehension Check

### Retell the Selection

Use the Retelling Cards to retell the selection.

**Retelling Cards**

| Activity | Kids in One Place | Kids in Another Place |
|---|---|---|
|  |  |  |

### Think and Compare

1. What is the same about how the boy and girl are helping to wash things? What is different?

2. How do you help your family at home?

3. How do kids in different places help like you do?

4. What do the children in *Kids Can Help* and "When Kids Play" do that is the same? What is different?

## Poetry

**Genre**
Poems use words in imaginative ways.

 **Literary Element**
Word Choice is important in a poem. Poets often choose interesting words to write about everyday things.

 Find out more about kids around the world at www.macmillanmh.com

# Poems by Kids

Kids everywhere write poetry. These kids found new ways to write about the sky, the sea, and the sun.

# The Sky is Busy

The lighthouse
On that island
Is shining.
Helicopters in the sky
Are shining.
Boats are glittering, too.
And with a bang
Someone is shooting
off fireworks.
Today the sky
Is very busy.

Ishikawa Mwumi,
Kindergarten, Japan

# The Sea

The mist smudges out
Kapiti Island

the hills curve and rise
like loaves of bread

the sun sprinkles glitter
on the sea

the wind is writing what it knows
in lines along the water.

Laura Ranger, age 7,
New Zealand

# Sun Rise

Sun, sun, sun
Rise up from the clouds
Spread your rays
Flowers will be happy
Birds will sing
And I shall be happy
and sing, too.

Camille Pabalan,
age 6, Canada

## Connect and Compare

Choose a child from *Kids Can Help*. What might this child write a poem about?

Some **verbs** tell about actions that happen now.

# Write About Helping

Michael wrote about helping at home.

I like the book <u>Kids Can Help</u>.

I like to cook.

The boy in the book cooks, too.

# ISTEP+ Writing Activity

What did you learn from <u>Kids Can Help</u>?

Write about how you help at home.

## Writer's Checklist

☑ Did I write some short sentences and some long ones?

☑ Did I use verbs that tell what happens now?

☑ Did I underline the book title?

## Talk About It

What is a shadow? What kind of shadows can you make?

 Find out more about shadows at **www.macmillanmh.com**

# Me and My Shadow

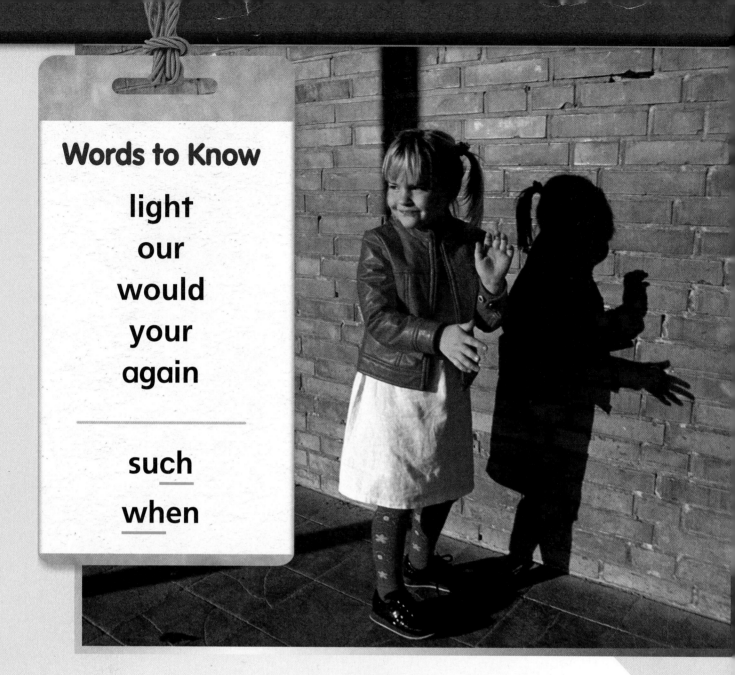

**Words to Know**

light
our
would
your
again

such
when

# Light Game

We can play with **light**. Look at
**our** hands. We can make shapes.
It's such fun! We play when the
sun is up.

**Would** you like to play? Use **your** hands. Use the sun. Make some shapes. You can play **again** and again.

# Short Shadows, Long Shadows

### What makes your shadow get big and little?

**Our** shadows walk with us. They jump with us. But they change in ways that we do not.

**Light** makes shadows. When
light hits you, a shadow falls.

**Your** shadow can be long or
short. What makes this happen?

When light changes, shadows do too. Light from the sun changes all day. When you wake up, the sun is low. It makes a long shadow.

When you eat lunch, the sun is way up in the sky. Now, the sun makes short shadows.

The sun looks like it moves.
But it does not. Earth does.

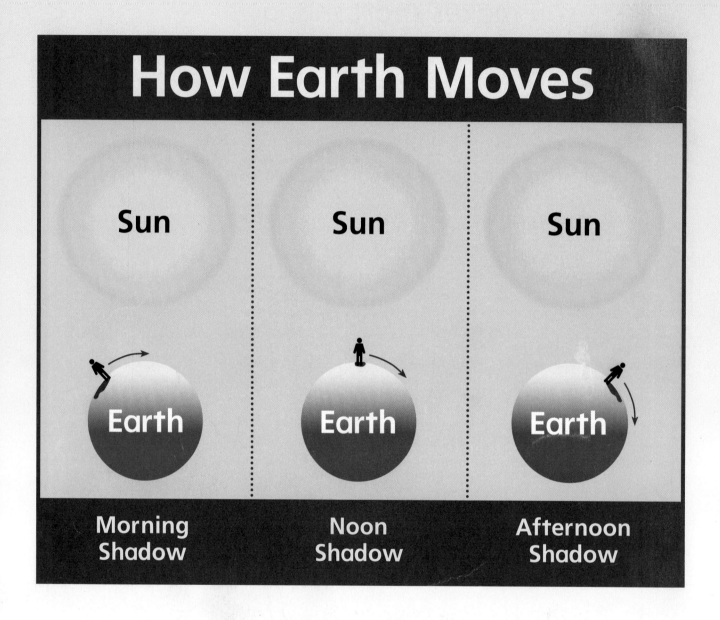

## How Earth Moves

Sun

Sun

Sun

Earth

Earth

Earth

**Morning Shadow**

**Noon Shadow**

**Afternoon Shadow**

All day and night, Earth spins.
That makes the sun look like it
is going up and down.

In the afternoon, the sun gets
lower **again**. Look at these
shadows. Which **would** you see
in the late afternoon?

When would your shadow be very long? How could you get your shadow to be in back of you? Go out in the sun and check!

 **Comprehension Check**

## Tell What You Learned

What did you learn about shadows and the sun?

## Think and Compare

1. How do shadows change during the day?

2. How can you make shadows indoors?

3. Besides your own shadow, what shadows do you see? What are they like?

4. What time of day do you think would be the best to play the game in "Light Game"?

**Test Strategy**

**Think and Search**
Find the answer in more than one place.

Every morning, we see the sun come up. All day we see it up in the sky. It gives Earth light so people can see. It gives Earth heat.

Every afternoon, we see the sun go down. When the sun sets, it gets dark outside. Soon, it will be time to sleep.

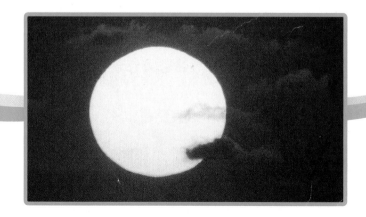

84

Go On

**ISTEP+**  **Numbers 1 to 3 are based on "The Sun."**

**1** What is the story MAINLY about?

○                    ○                    ○

**2** What does the sun give Earth?

○ It gives Earth heat and light.

○ It gives Earth dark and light.

○ It gives Earth sleep and sky.

**Tip**
Keep reading to find the answer.

**3** What is it time to do after the sun sets?

○ It is time to get warm.

○ It is time to eat lunch.

○ It is time to go to sleep.

STOP 85

# Write About Day and Night

Julie wrote about how the night looks.

## NIGHT

Night is dark.
The moon and stars shine.
They light up the dark sky.

**ISTEP+** # What Daytime Is Like

What does daytime look like?
What does it feel like?
Write three or more sentences
that describe daytime.

## Editing Checklist

1 Have you started each
sentence with a capital letter?

2 Have you ended each
sentence with the correct
mark?

3 Have you spelled all words
correctly?

# Our Families

## Talk About It

What is a family?
How are families
alike and different?

LOG ON  Find out more about
families at
www.macmillanmh.com

**Words to Know**

how

there

so

more

funny

call

———

t<u>i</u>m<u>e</u>

f<u>i</u>n<u>e</u>

**Read to Find Out**

Which dog will
Ike pick?

# A Funny Dog for Ike

by Linda B. Ross

illustrated by Anthony Lewis

91

 **Ike:** **How** will we pick out the best dog for us? **There** are **so** many dogs here!

 **Dad:** Let's take our time. We will see one that we like **more** than the rest.

 **Ike:** I like this **funny** little dog!
I think he likes me, too!

 **Mom:** Then this must be the one!

94

 **Mom:** He looks like a fine dog to me.

 **Ike:** Let's **call** him Wags!

95

# Comprehension

**Genre**
A play is a story that can be acted out.

**Ask Questions**
Make Predictions
As you read, use your **Predictions Chart.**

| What I Predict | What Happens |
|---|---|
|  |  |
|  |  |
|  |  |

**Read to Find Out**
Who will make Mike smile?

96

# Smile, Mike!
## A Play

Award
Winning
Illustrator

by Aida Marcuse

illustrated by G. Brian Karas

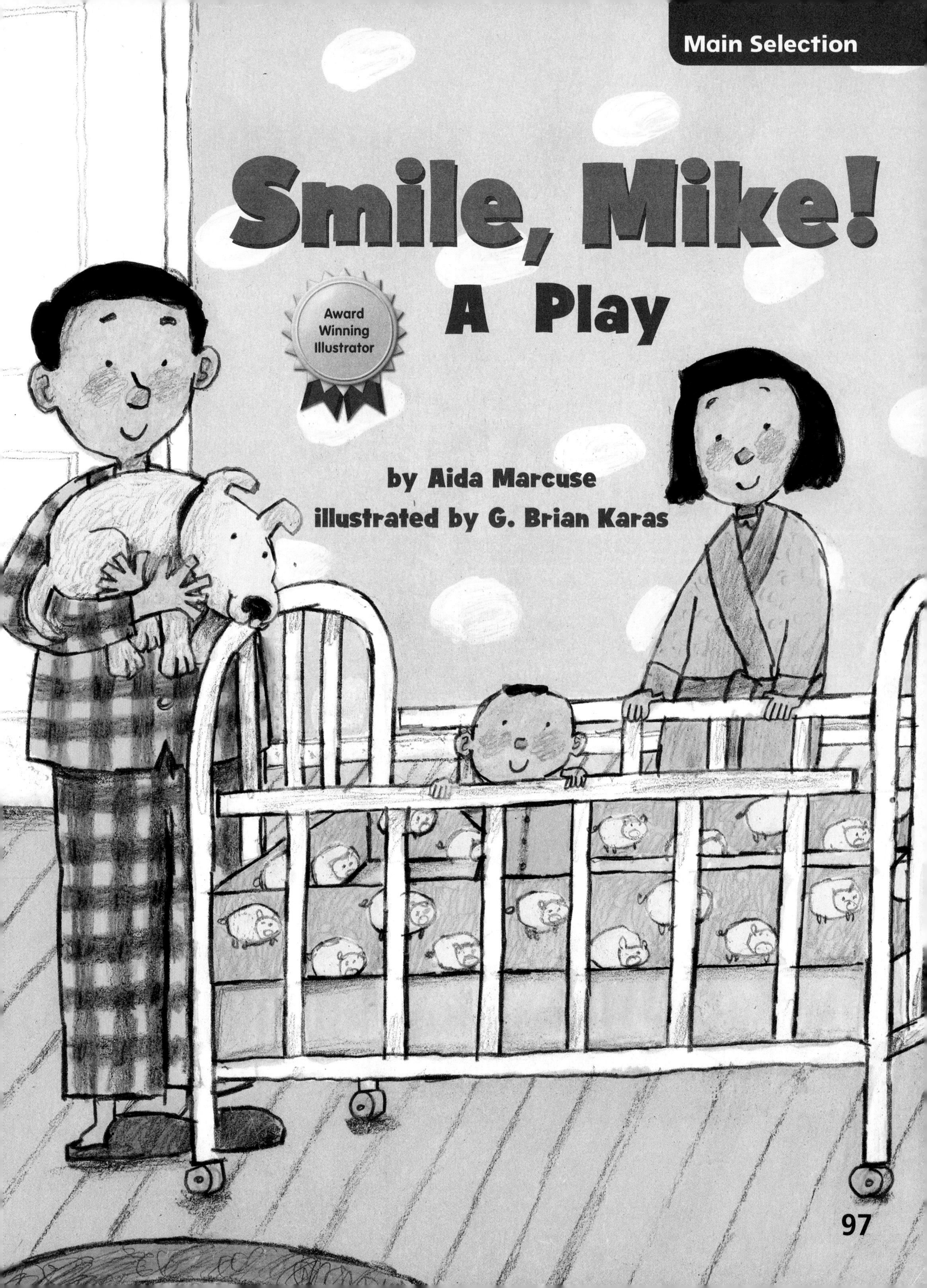

# Meet the Characters

 Mike

 Spike

 Juan

 Ana

 Mom

 Dad

 Gram

 Pops

**Mike:**  Wa! Wa! Wa!

**Mom:**  Here we are, Baby Mike.

**Dad:**  Did you **call** us? Are you hungry?

**Mom:**  No, he just had a fine snack.

 **Mike:** Wa! Wa! Wa!

 **Ana:** Why is Mike **so** sad?

 **Juan:** Let's make him happy.
Do you want this cat, Mike?

 **Mike:** No! No! No cat!

100

 **Ana:** Let's sing. **A - B - C - D - E - F - G - H - I -**

 **Dad:** **J - K - L - M - N - O - P -**

 **Juan:** **Q - R - S - T - U - V - W - X - Y - Z.**

 **Mike:** No! No! No sing!

 **Gram:** Why is our little Mike so sad?

 **Mike:** Wa! Wa! Wa!

 **Pops:** **How** can we make him smile?

 **Gram:** Let's clap hands!

 **Pops:** Clap with us, Mike.

 **Mike:** Wa! Wa! Wa!

 **Gram:** Clap hands with us.

 **Mike:** No! No! No clap!

 **Ana:** My **funny** duck will make Mike smile.

 **Mike:** Wa! Wa! Wa!

**Mom:** Do not whine, Mike. Quack with us. Quack! Quack!

**Mike:** No! No! No quack!

**Dad:**　Look, Mike! I can make bubbles!

**Mike:**　Wa! Wa! Wa!

**Gram:**　And I can catch a little bubble.

**Mike:**　No! No! No bubbles!

 **Ana:** Mike, look at my funny duck.

 **Mike:** Wa! Wa! Wa!

 **Juan:** And look at my little cat.

 **Gram:** Look at me, Mike.

 **Mike:** Wa! Wa! Wa!

 **Dad:** Look! **There** are **more** bubbles!

 **Pops:** Look, Mike! There is Spike.

 **Mike:** Wa! Wa! Wa!

 **Juan:** Did you come to see Mike, Spike?

 **Ana:** Spike wants to make Mike smile.

 **Gram:** Look at Spike spin.

 **Ana:** Spike is funny!

 **Gram:** Look! Mike has a big smile.

 **Pops:** Spike made Mike smile.

**Juan:** Good dog! This is for you, Spike.

**Dad:** Show us how you can jump.

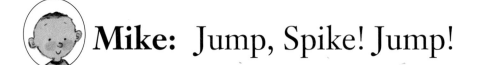**Mike:** Jump, Spike! Jump!

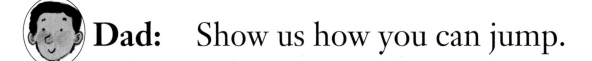**Spike:** Ruff! Ruff!

 **Dad:** At last, Mike is happy.

 **Mom:** Now it is time for bed.

 **Ana:** Mike will get some rest now.

 **Gram:** And so will we!

# Smile with Aida Marcuse!

**Aida Marcuse** says, "I wrote *Smile, Mike!* because mothers always try to make their children happy. I remember the day when my little boy wouldn't stop crying. At last we discovered what he wanted! I hope you enjoy reading this play. I enjoyed writing it!"

**LOG ON** Find out more about Aida Marcuse at **www.macmillanmh.com**

## Write About It

In Aida Marcuse's play, Mike smiles. Write about what makes someone in your family smile.

# Comprehension Check

## Retell the Story

Use the Retelling Cards to retell the story.

**Retelling Cards**

## Think and Compare

| What I Predict | What Happens |
| --- | --- |
|  |  |
|  |  |
|  |  |

1. What do you think Mike's family will do the next time he cries?

2. How is Mike's family like your family?

3. What are some other ways you can make a baby smile and laugh?

4. How is Wags in "A Funny Dog for Ike" like Spike?

# Family Fun

Who lives with you?
Who is in your family?

Come and meet
two kids and their
families!

My name is Matt. I live with my mom, my dad, and my brother, Rick. My **aunt** Kate and my **grandfather** live with us, too.

We all go to the park to play ball. I like to hit. Rick likes to catch. He is good!

My name is Carmen. I live with my mom and **grandmother**.

We have so much fun together. We like to make up funny songs. We act them out, too!

This chart shows Matt's family and Carmen's family. How are they the same? How are they different?

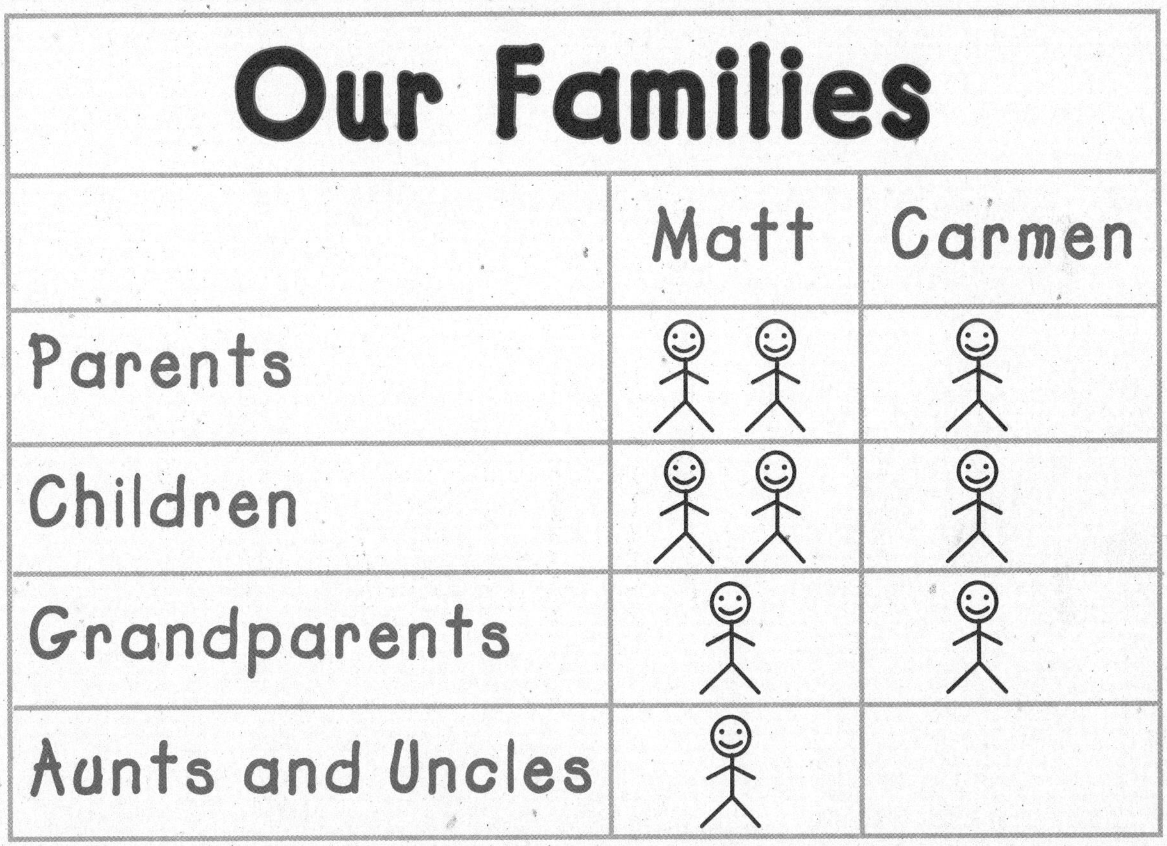

## Our Families

| | Matt | Carmen |
|---|---|---|
| Parents | 🙂🙂 | 🙂 |
| Children | 🙂🙂 | 🙂 |
| Grandparents | 🙂 | 🙂 |
| Aunts and Uncles | 🙂 | |

**Connect and Compare**

Think about the family in *Smile, Mike!* If you could add them to the chart, what would it look like?

# Make a Poster

Amy made a poster
about a play.

Grade 1 is in a play.

It is <u>Smile, Mike!</u>

We are so funny!

Come see it.

118

 # Writing Activity

What kind of play could your class put on?

Think of a play and make a poster about it.

## Writer's Checklist

☑ Is my poster easy to read?

☑ Did I use the verbs *is* and *are* correctly?

☑ Does my exclamation end with an exclamation mark?

# Family Time

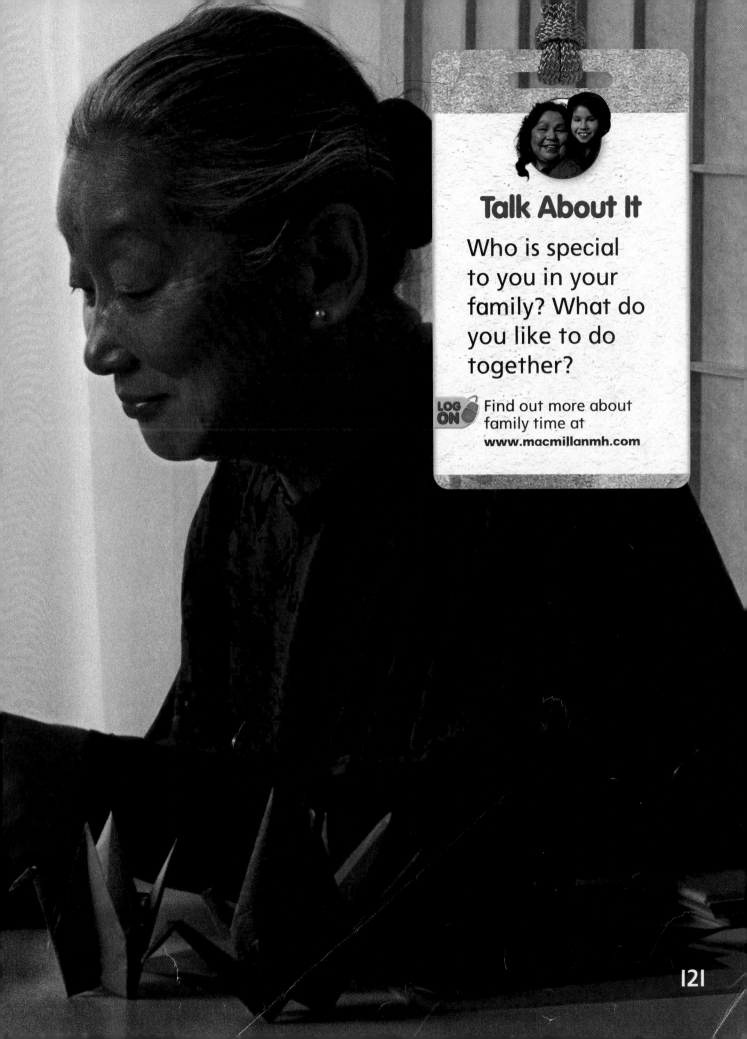

## Talk About It

Who is special to you in your family? What do you like to do together?

**LOG ON** Find out more about family time at **www.macmillanmh.com**

## Words to Know

give
were
say
about
read
says

---

spring
stretches

122

# What I Like About Spring

by Ellen Bruce

illustrated by Lizzy Rockwell

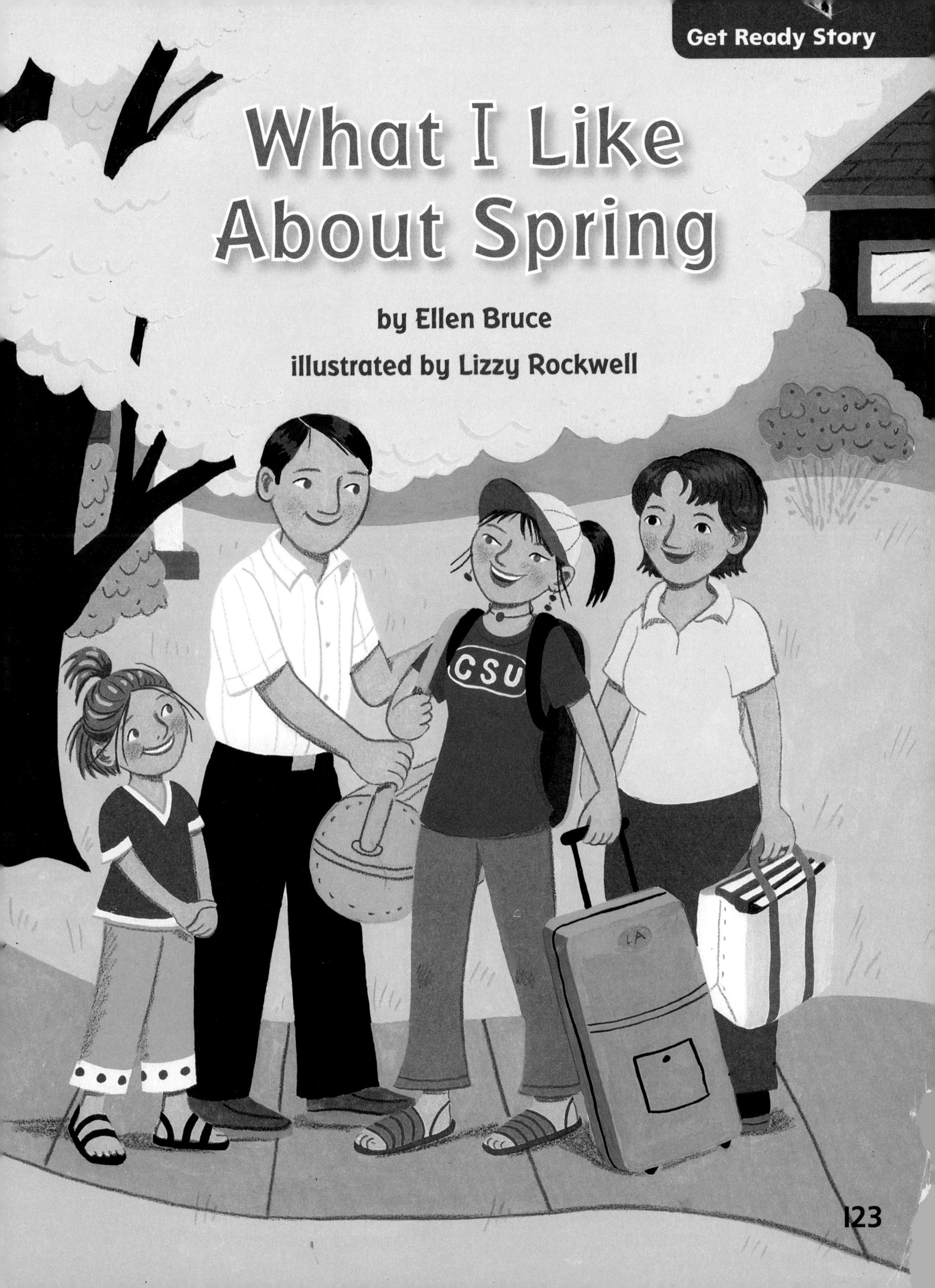

In the spring, Liz comes back to live with us. Mom and Dad and I are so glad to see her.

Liz picks me up.
I **give** her a big kiss.

"You **were** away for so long!"
I **say**.

Liz tells me all **about** her school.
She has to **read** a lot!

"Let's play now," Liz **says**. "Jump up."

I get on. Liz stretches and spins.

I am so glad Liz is back. I like spring!

## Comprehension

### Genre

**Realistic Fiction** is a made-up story that could really happen.

### Ask Questions
**Character and Setting**
As you read, use your **Character and Setting Chart.**

| What the Characters Do | Where They Do It |
|---|---|
|  |  |

**Read to Find Out**
What do Gram and James do together?

128

# Gram and Me

by Miriam Cohen

illustrated by Floyd Cooper

Award Winning
**Author**
and
**Illustrator**

I like my grandmother a lot.
I call her Gram.
She is so much fun.

Gram takes me fishing.
We sit together on the dock.
We wave at the boats.
"Hello!" we call.

Gram helps me ride my bike.
She is strong.
"You can do it, James!" she **says**.
"Look at me go!" I **say**.

Gram has a big, striped cat.
His name is Scruff.
"Scratch him under the chin," she says.
"Scruff likes it!" I say.

Gram likes to play chess.
She helps me when we play.
"Think, James," she says.
"I win, Gram!" I say.

Gram has a lot of spring flowers.
She lets me **give** them a drink.
"Flowers like a good drink," she says.
"Look! They drank it all up," I say.

Gram has a big plum tree.
We like to pick plums.
Gram lifts me up.
"I got a ripe one!" I say.

Gram shows me how to make plum jam.
She adds salt to the pot.
"Just a bit," she says.
"Yum! This jam will taste good!" I say.

"Gram, did you cook when you **were** little?" I ask.

"I helped my mom," says Gram. "We made jam just like you and I do."

"Did you go to school?" I ask.
"Yes, I went to a little school," says Gram.
"My school is very big," I say.
"Yes, it is," says Gram.

"I am learning how to **read** at school,"
I say.
"Reading is good," says Gram. "I liked
to read when I was little."
"Gram, can you read me a story?"

"Yes," says Gram. "Do you like cats and dogs?"
"I like them a lot!" I say.
"This is a story **about** cats and dogs."

143

I like Gram's story a lot.
"Let's read more," I say.
"Can you read a story to me?" asks Gram.
"I think I can."

"I will read you this story," I say.
"Is it about cats and dogs?" Gram asks.
"No, it is a story about pigs."
"Pigs are good, too," says Gram.

"This is a story about three little pigs," I say.
I read on and on.

At the end, Gram claps and claps.
"What a fine story," she says.
"Gram, you are so much fun," I say.
"So are you," says my Gram.

# We Remember Gram

**Miriam Cohen** says, "I wrote this story about a grandma because I loved mine so much. She told me stories about when she was a girl."

**Another book by Miriam Cohen**

**Floyd Cooper** says, "I loved my gram's gingerbread. I start my paintings by spreading gingerbread-colored paint on paper. So, I remember Gram every time I make a painting!"

**LOG ON** Find out more about Miriam Cohen and Floyd Cooper at **www.macmillanmh.com**

**Another book by Floyd Cooper**

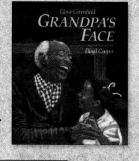

## Write About It

Write about someone in your family. Tell what you do together.

## Comprehension Check

### Retell the Story

Use the Retelling Cards to retell the story.

**Retelling Cards**

### Think and Compare

| What the Characters Do | Where They Do It |
|---|---|
|  |  |

1. What does James like to do with Gram?

2. What do you like to do with an older relative?

3. What can kids learn from older relatives?

4. How are James and the little sister in "What I Like About Spring" alike?

# CELEBRATE Chinese New Year

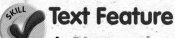
Happy New Year! This is how people **celebrate** Chinese New Year.

## Things to Do

1. Help cook.

2. Make a costume.

3. Get a flag.

4. Get gifts.

To get set for the Chinese New Year, Ming Lee makes a list. She has a lot to do!

To celebrate, people go to see **relatives**. They give gifts. Kids get red packets with money in them. They have good things to eat like New Year's cake.

Chinese New Year ends in a big **parade**. People dress up. They wave big flags. What a great start to a new year!

**Connect and Compare**

How might James and Gram from *Gram and Me* celebrate the new year?

# Write About a Relative

Joey wrote about his grandpa.

My grandpa doesn't like to drive. He likes to walk.

One time we walked two miles! We weren't even tired.

# Writing Activity

Which older relative do you like to spend time with?

Write what you like to do together.

## Writer's Checklist

☑ Did I use my best handwriting?

☑ Did I form contractions correctly?

☑ Did I use an apostrophe in my contractions?

# Let's Go!

**Characters**

Abby          Amy

Abby

I am your babysitter today.

Amy

What will we do?

Abby

I want to ride my bike.

Amy

I want to go to the park.

Go On

Abby

But I am the babysitter!

Amy

I have an idea. Let's ride bikes.

Abby

That is what I want to do!

Amy

Let's ride to the park.

Abby

Good thinking. Let's go!

# Answer Questions

**Tip**

Look for the answer.

 **Numbers 1 to 3 are based on "Let's Go!"**

**1** What does Abby want to do?

    ○             ○             ○

**2** What is Amy's idea?

   ○ to go for a walk

   ◉ to ride to the park

   ○ to play with a friend

**3** What will Abby and Amy do?

   ○ put their bikes away

   ○ play in the house

   ◉ ride their bikes to the park

Go On ➡

**ISTEP+ My Favorite Activity**

What is your favorite thing to do with a family member or babysitter? Tell about it.

Write three or more sentences.

**STOP** 157

# Glossary

## What is a Glossary?

A glossary can help you find the meanings of words. The words are listed in alphabetical order. You can look up a word and read it in a sentence. There is a picture to help you.

## Sample Entry

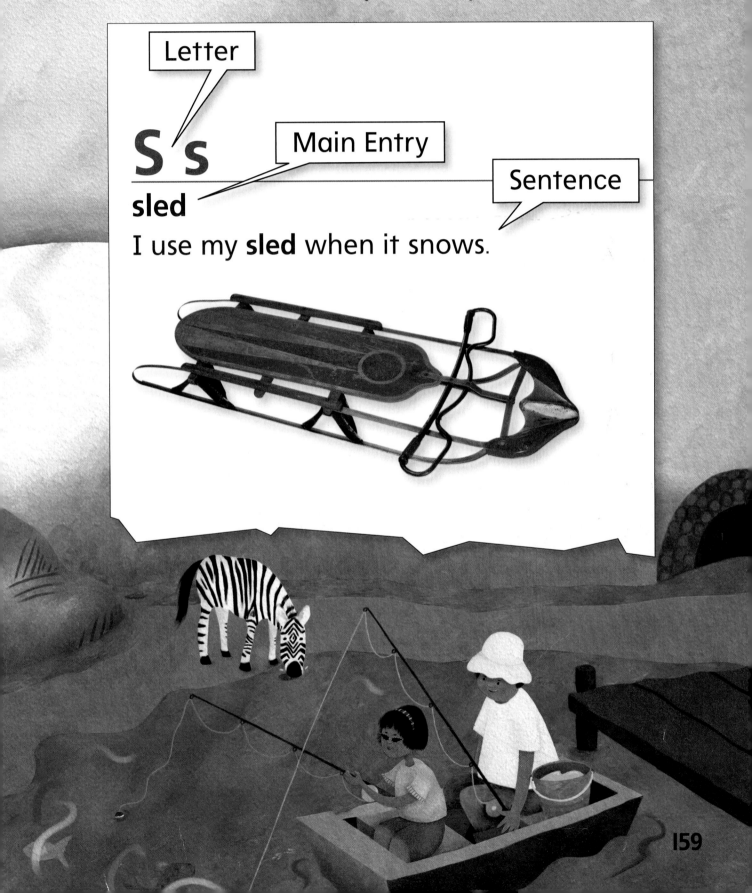

Letter

Main Entry

Sentence

**S s**

**sled**

I use my **sled** when it snows.

# Bb

**baby**

The **baby** has a toy.

**bubbles**

The **bubbles** are colorful.

# Cc

**catch**

I **catch** the ball.

# Dd

**dock**

The boat is tied to the **dock**.

# Ff

**flowers**

The **flowers** are pretty.

# Ll

**letter**

I mail a **letter** to my grandma.

**llama**

This **llama** lives in the mountains.

# Pp

---

**path**

We walk on the **path**.

**pull**

I **pull** this wagon.

# Rr

**rake**

We **rake** the leaves.

**river**

This **river** is long.

# Ss

**sled**

I use my **sled** when it snows.

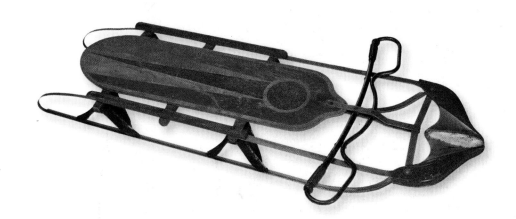

**striped**

A zebra is **striped**.

**suds**

This bath has **suds**.

# Tt

**together**

Katie and Matt build **together**.

**tossed**

Ms. Clare **tossed** the ball to Rosa.

# Acknowledgments

*The publisher gratefully acknowledges permission to reprint the following copyrighted material:*

"The Sky is Busy" by Ishikawa Megumi © 1993 from *Festival in My Heart: Poems by Japanese Children*, Harry N. Abrams, Incorporated, NY, A Times Mirror Corporations, Reprinted with permission from Harry N. Abrams, Inc, NY

"The Sea" by Laura Ranger from poems from Stone Soup Magazine May/June 1993 issue. © 2005 Stone Soup, Santa Cruz, CA 95063

"Sun Rise" by Camille Pabalan from KidzPage: Poetry and Verse for Children of All Ages, November 2000, page 36 Tangled Lives, © 1998 – 2000, Emmi Tarr

Book Cover, ALTOONA BABOONA by Janie Bynum. Copyright © 2002 by Janie Bynum. Reprinted by permission of Voyager Books.

Book Cover, OTIS by Janie Bynum. Copyright © 2000 by Janie Bynum. Reprinted by permission of Harcourt Children's Books.

Book Cover, WHEN WILL I READ? by Miriam Cohen, illustrated by Lillian Hoban. Text copyright © 1977 by Miriam Cohen. Illustrations Copyright © 1977 by Lillian Hoban. Reprinted by permission of Greenwillow Books.

Book Cover, GRANDPA'S FACE by Eloise Greenfield, illustrated by Floyd Cooper. Text copyright © 1996 by Eloise Greenfield. Illustrations copyright © 1996 by Floyd Cooper. Reprinted by permission of Penguin Putnam Books for Young Readers.

**ILLUSTRATION**
**Cover Illustration:** Jerry LoFaro

8-13: Daniel Moreton. 14-29: Janie Bynum. 36: John Hovell. 38: Liz Callen. 48–49: Claude Martinot. 64-65: Claude Martinot. 66-69: Tomek Bogacki. 80: Rick Nease for TFK. 90-95: Anthony Lewis. 96-111: G. Brian Karas. 118: Liz Callen. 122-127: Lizzy Rockwell. 128-145: Floyd Cooper. 154-157: Elivia Savadier. 158-167: Janee Trasler.

**PHOTOGRAPHY**
*All Photographs are by Macmillan/McGraw Hill (MMH) except as noted below:*

6-7: Bruno De Hogues/Getty Images, Inc. 7: (tr) Barbara Penoyar/Getty Images, Inc. 30: Courtesy Janie Bynum. 32-33: Ken Karp. 34: (l) Geri Engberg/The Image Works, Inc.; (r) Robyn Beck/AFP/Getty Images, Inc. 35: (b) Torsten Maiwald; (r),(c) Ken Karp. 36: Ken Karp. 38: LWA-Dann Tardif/CORBIS. 39: (t),(b) PhotoDisc/Getty Images, Inc.

40-41: Chris Arend /Alaska Stock Images. 41: (tr) Ingo Jezierski/Getty Images, Inc. 42: (br) Wendy Stone/CORBIS; (tr) Alex Griffiths/Alamy. 43: Tony Anderson/Taxi/Getty Images, Inc. 44: AP-Wide World Photos. 45: Michael St. Maur Sheil/CORBIS. 46: Ron Gilling/Lineair/Peter Arnold, Inc. 47: (tl) Ariel Skelley/CORBIS; (tr) Michael S. Yamashita/CORBIS; (bc) Steve Skjold/Alamy. 48-49: Rachel LaCour Niesen/IPN. 50: Tom & Dee Ann McCarthy/CORBIS. 51: Paul Chesley/Stone/Getty Images, Inc. 52: Paul A. Souders/CORBIS. 53: van hilversum/Alamy. 54: Robert Maust/Photo Agora. 55: Cundy/Alamy. 56: FSG/AGE Fotostock America. 57: Bjorn Svensson/AGE Fotostock. 58: B&C Alexander/Arctic Photos. 59: Robert Frerck/Odyssey. Productions. 60: David Morris/Alamy. 61: Barry Runk/Grant Heilman Photography. 62: Bob Daemmrich/The Image Works, Inc. 63: Richard Levine/Alamy. 64: Courtesy of Minda Novek. 70: (l) Thinkstock/Alamy; (r) Foodfolio/Alamy; (c) CheapShots/Alamy. 71: (l) Ingram Publishing/Alamy; (r) Cheapshots/Alamy. 72-73: Image Source/Index Stock Imagery. 74: plainpicture/Alamy. 75: Bonnie Kamin/Photo Edit Inc. 76: (cl) David Young-Wolff/Photo Edit Inc.; (tc) Creatas/Punchstock. 77: SSPL/The Image Works. 78: (c) Bill Brooks/Masterfile; (cr) CORBIS/Punchstock. 79: Claudia Kunin/CORBIS. 81: (t) Liane Cary/Age Fotostock; (cr) Norbert Schaefer/CORBIS. 82: SHOUT/Alamy. 84: Dynamic Graphics Group/Creatas/Alamy. 85: (tl) Photodisc/Getty Images, Inc.; (tl) Digistock/Alamy; (tc) Courtesy NASA. 86: Angelo Cavalli/AGE Fotostock. 87: (c), (cr) Dian Lofton for TFK; (bcr) C Squared Studios/Photodisc/Getty Images, Inc. 88-89: Myrleen Ferguson Cate/Photo Edit Inc. 89: (tr) Jack Hollingsworth/Getty Images, Inc. 112: Courtesy Aida Marcuse. 114: (l) Brand X Pictures/Getty Images, Inc.; (r) Michael Keller/CORBIS. 115: (c) Michael Keller/CORBIS. 116: Brand X Pictures/Getty Images, Inc. 118: Dynamic Graphics Group/Creatas/Alamy. 119: (t) Hemera Technologies/Alamy; (b) Photodisc/Getty Images, Inc. 120-121: Walter Hodges/Getty Images, Inc. 121: (tr) Barbara Penoyar/Getty Images, Inc. 146: (cl) Courtesy Floyd Cooper; (tr) Courtesy Miriam Cohen. 148: A. Ramey/Photo Edit Inc. 149: (t) Laura Dwight/Omni-Photo Communications Inc.; (b) Brand X Pictures/Picture Quest. 150: (bl) Michael Newman/Photo Edit Inc.; (br) Phil Schermeister/CORBIS; (t) Lawrence Migdale/PIX. 151: (l) Ted Streshinsky/CORBIS; (r) Nik Wheeler/CORBIS. 152: Pedro Coll/AGE Fotostock America. 153: COMSTOCK/Getty Images, Inc. 159: Siede Preis/Getty Images, Inc. 160: (t) Paul Loven/The Image Bank/Getty Images, Inc.; (b) Bill Hickey/The Image Bank/Getty Images, Inc. 162: C Squared Studios/Getty Images, Inc. 163: Andre Jenny/Alamy. 164: Thinkstock/Getty Images, Inc. 165: (t) James Marshall/CORBIS; (b) Siede Preis/Getty Images, Inc. 166: (t) Ryan McVay/Getty Images, Inc.; (b) Michael Keller/CORBIS. 167: Bananastock/Alamy.